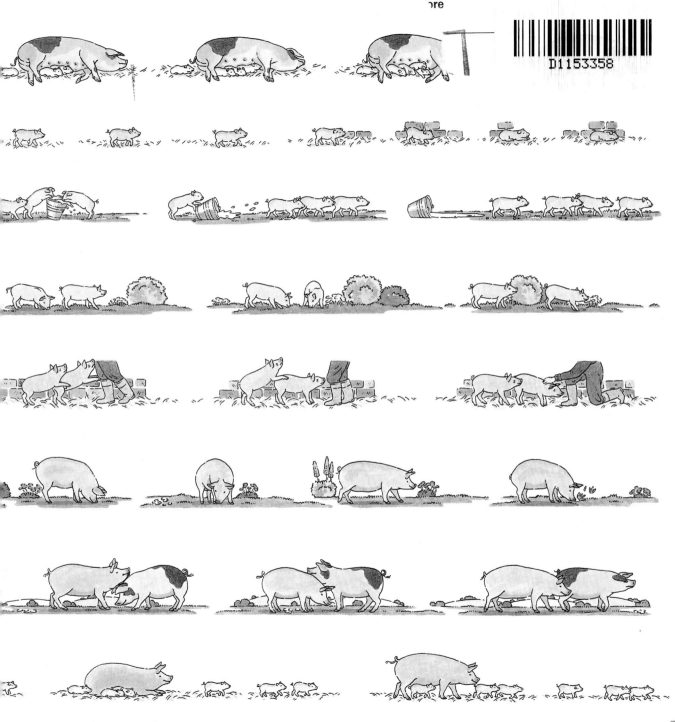

PET

A DORLING KINDERSLEY BOOK

Written and edited by Mary Ling
Art Editor Helen Senior
Production Shelagh Gibson
Illustrator Jane Cradock-Watson
Additional photography Tim Ridley

Special thanks to Mike Sherren and his pigs

First published in Great Britain in 1993 by
Dorling Kindersley Limited, 9 Henrietta Street, London WC2E 8PS

A CIP catalogue record for this book is available
from the British Library

ISBN 0-7513-5002-8

Colour reproduction by J. Film Ltd, Singapore
Printed in Italy by L.E.G.O.

SEE HOW THEY GROW
PIG

photographed by
BILL LING

DORLING KINDERSLEY
London • New York • Stuttgart

Pink and new

I am a piglet. I have just
been born. So have
my six brothers
and sisters.

We squeak and
squeal because
we are wet and
cold. Our legs
are very wobbly.

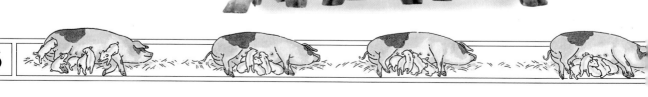

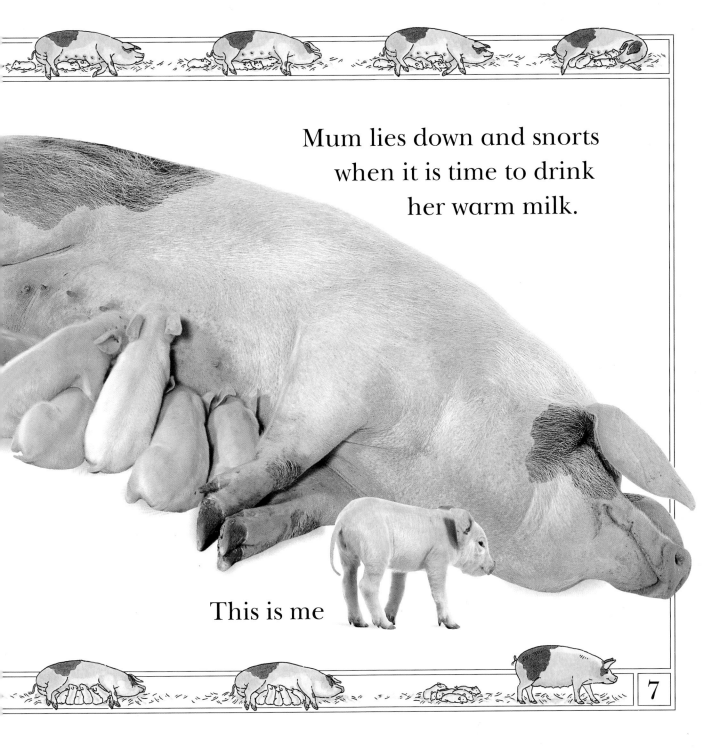

Mum lies down and snorts
when it is time to drink
her warm milk.

This is me

Sleepy piglets

I am two days
old and my
ears get bigger
every day.

My sister wants to
play with me. But
I am cosy here.

Sometimes the cold
wind blows into
our sty. We all
snuggle together
to keep warm.

Trotting around

Today we are two weeks old. We are trotting around the farmyard. Here comes the farmer. Let's follow him to the gate.

Big pigs

I am six weeks old. So are
my brothers and sisters.

We feed
from the
trough,
just like
the big
pigs.

Am I as big as mum yet?
No. Not quite.

When I am
sleepy, I make a soft
nest out of straw.

Mud pies

I am six months old now and I am getting chubby. I like playing in the mud.

We find tasty things to eat there. The mud is cool and sploshy.

A yellow bucket

I am one year old. It is winter
and my trotters are very
 mucky. What is this?

The farmer has left
his bucket behind.
I wonder what is inside.

It is empty.
Oh well ...
it is nearly
time for
supper.

A new mum

I am one and a half years old.
I have eight little piglets of
my own to care for now.

They are very tiny. I am careful not to step on them. Soon they will grow big and strong just like me.

See how I grew

Newborn   Two days old   Two weeks old   Six weeks old

Six months old   One year old

One and a half years old

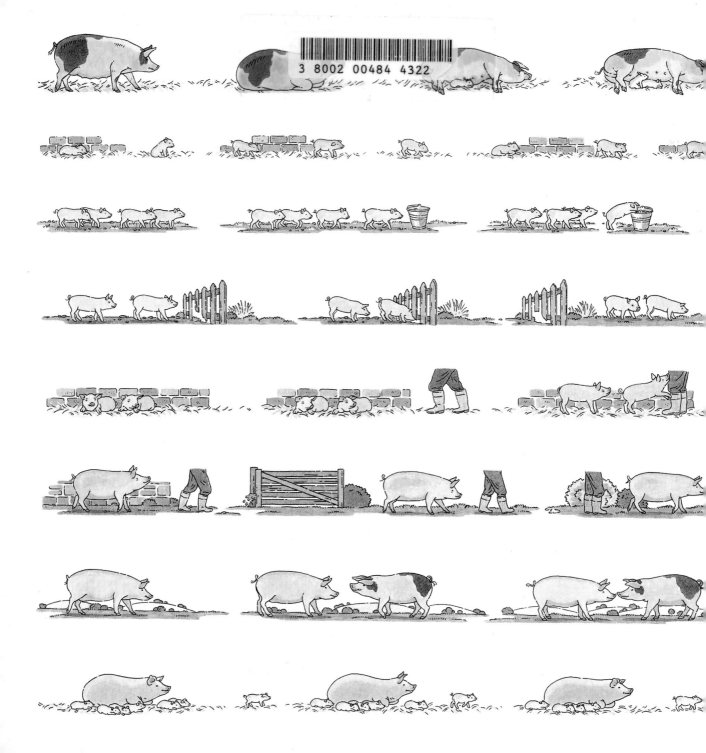